Home

Welcome home to The Mississippi Delta.

A RECIPE STORY BOOK WRITTEN BY DELTA FOLK, FOR DELTA FOLK.

Spirts by Erskine Moore
Meals by Cameron Shaw
Dessert Contribution by Jace Swims

Illustrations and Flash Fiction by Erica Sandifer

Contents

Delta Woman,
Dammit Part Two

Here lies heaven and the underworld beneath and between, Most the men loved a Delta woman 'cos they pretty, can cook and real damn mean,

Plus, she can dance the shucks off an ear of corn way down by the cornfields, Spitting sunflower seeds running through the Carroll County foothills,

Ain't got much time for the church women and their judgements,

Ain't no time for the brothers that only want to put buns in her oven,

Can't say soul without saying a Delta Lady's name,

Get the taste slapped out yo' mouth for using the Lord's name in vain,

The winter gone come—so she's canning garden tomatoes,

Until then she's sleeping with her panties on because of Delta tornadoes, She don't go wherever the wind blow and that's a natural born fact,

Damn show don't like no weak man—crying and begging to come back, She still going to church on Sunday dressed like the preacher's daughter, At the juke joint Friday night dancing to the blues like the devil taught her, But it's all okay 'cos she knows God knows her heart,

She a Delta woman, they all get off to a rough start....

SPIRITS

The Cleveland

1 oz. Campari

1 oz. Sweet Vermouth

1 oz. Bulleit Rye

Pour ingredients over ice and garnish with orange peel.

Highway 61

2 oz. Tequila

1/2 oz. Triple Sec

1/2 oz. Simple Syrup

2 oz. Pink Lemonade

Instructions: Shake. Strain over ice.

Sand Water

1 oz. Malibu Rum

1/2 oz. Bacardi Rum

1/2 oz. Blue Curacao

1 oz. Pineapple Juice

1 oz. Sweet and Sour

Instructions: Stir. Float 1/2 oz. 151 Rum on top.

Delta Iced Tea

2 oz. Sweet Tea Vodka

1 oz. Lemon Juice

1 oz. Sweet and Sour

1 oz. Sweet Tea

Instructions: Shake. Strain over ice. Garnish with lemon wedge.

Leflore County

1/2 oz. Vodka

1/2 oz. Midori

1/2 oz. Apple Pucker

1/2 oz. Watermelon Pucker

Instructions: Fill glass with half pineapple, half cranberry juice. Pour ingredients over ice.

Bea Louise

1 oz. Malibu Rum

1/2 oz. Blue Curacao

2 oz. Pineapple Juice

1 oz. Orange Juice

Instructions: Shake. Pour over glass of ice.

A Southerner's Dream

2 – 3 Fresh Strawberries

1/2 oz. Simple Syrup

1 1/2 oz. Smirnoff Strawberry Vodka

2 oz. Lemonade

Instructions: Muddle strawberries and simple syrup in shaker glass. Add lemonade and vodka. Shake and strain over crushed ice. Top with strawberry wine.

Greenwood Goddamn

2 oz. Buffalo Trace Bourbon

1/2 oz. Pineapple Juice

1 oz. Sweet Vermouth

2 Dashes of bitters

Instructions: Shake. Pour over ice.

Mississippi Sunday

1 oz. Crème De Banana

2 oz. Sweet and Sour

1 1⁄2 oz Bacardi Rum

Instructions: Blend with ice.

The Boat

1 oz. Smirnoff Grape

1 oz. Smirnoff Vodka

2 oz. Cranberry Juice

Instructions: Stir. Pour over ice.

SALADS

Cornfield Salad

2 Roasted Corn on the Cobs 1/2
Cup Cherry Tomatoes

1/4 Cup of Red Onions

1/4 Cup of Feta Cheese

1/4 Roasted Cauliflower

Field Dressing

1/2 Cup of Sour Cream

1/2 Cup of Buttermilk

2 tbs of Minced Garlic

Salt & pepper to taste

2 tbs of Parsley

2 tbs Lemon Juice

1 tbs of Hot Sauce

2 tbs of Chopped Mint

Preset grill to 350 degrees. Rub both corn shucks with unsalted butter. Add a pinch of salt and pepper until corn is covered. Gently rub in one tbsp's of minced garlic on the ear of corn before grilling. Boil cauliflower in a large pot of water over medium heat for 6-8 minutes to soften. Drain water from cauliflower. Remove pan. Repeat the same method with cauliflower as the corn on the cob. Grill cauliflower and corn until they both have grill marks. Let cool. After cooling, shuck roasted corn on the cob into a large bowl. Add cherry tomatoes, red onions, and roasted cauliflower. Thoroughly mix together. Scoop into a large bowl.

Dressing

In a medium bowl, add sour cream, minced garlic, parsley, and mint together. Pour in buttermilk, lemon juice, and hot sauce. Stir ingredients together with large spoon, add salt and pepper to taste. Drizzle dressing on top of salad.

Garden Farm Cobb Salad

2 Cups of Baby Spinach

1/4 Cup of Bacon

1/4 Cup of Rooted Carrots

1/4 Cup of Goat Cheese

1/4 Cup of Grilled Chicken Breast

1/4 Cup of Heirloom Chopped Tomato

Garden Dressing

1/2 Cup of Vinegar

1/2 Cup of Canola Oil

¼ Cup of Minced Garlic Salt & Pepper to taste

1 tsp of Fresh Basil

2 tbs of Honey

1 tsp of Dijon Mustard

Place baby spinach in a large bowl. Grill chicken with salt, pepper, garlic, and olive oil. After grilling, place chicken to cool. Render 2 slices of bacon until crispy under a medium heat. Place an even layer of fresh goat cheese, sliced rooted carrots, diced tomatoes, diced bacon, and diced chicken until the whole bowl is covered toppings.

Pour vinegar, canola oil, Dijon mustard and honey into a large mason jar. Mince 1 to 2 fresh basil leaves and garlic. Add into jar. Shake until well mixed.

BLT Salad

1 Whole Sliced Tomato

½ Blue Cheese Crumbles

4 Sliced Thick Cuts of Bacon (cook rendered) ¼ Diced Red Onions

1 Grilled Stock of Romaine Lettuce

Place romaine on a large sized plate. Cut 1 large tomato into 6 ½ inch slices. In a medium sized pan, render bacon until crispy. Roughly chop bacon and dice red onion to ½ an inch. Cut head of romaine in half. Season with salt, pepper, and olive oil. Grill romaine until there are light grill marks. Place blue cheese, red onions, and bacon on top of tomatoes. Serve!

Roasted Pear & Pecan Salad

¼ Blue Cheese

1 Roasted Pear

½ Half Cup Roasted Pecans 2 Cups of Baby Spinach

Citrus Dressing

1 Cup of Orange Juice ¼ Cup of Canola Oil ½ Cup of Honey

Set oven to 275 degrees. Cut and season pear with brown sugar. Cook pear for 15-20 minutes. Cool to room temperature. Season pecans with a pinch of salt, pepper, brown sugar, paprika, and olive oil. Roast pecans until light brown. Add citrus dressing to a cup of oranges in a small bowl. Add canola oil, honey, salt, and pepper to taste. Place baby spinach in a serving bowl. Top with roasted pecans, blue cheese, and roasted pears. Drizzle dressing on top of salad.

Money Road Green Bean Salad

1 lb. of Green Beans

1/3 Cup of Parmesan

1/2 Cup of Red Onions

1 Cup of Rendered Cubed Bacon

Dressing

1/4 Cup of Lemon Juice

1/4 Cup of Canola Oil

1 tbs of Garlic

Salt & Pepper to Taste

In large pot, boil water to a medium heat. Blanch greens for 2-3 minutes. Place in ice water until cool.

In a medium sized pan, render bacon until lightly crispy. Use leftover bacon grease to sauté red onions. Drain any excess grease. In a small bowl, toss dressing. Place green beans on a serving platter. Top with onions and bacon. Pour dressing on to bean salad. Serve!

SOUPS

Tomato Herb Garlic Bisque

12-15 Vine Tomatoes

6 Roasted Whole Cloves of Garlic

1 tbs Dry Basil

1 tbs Oregano

1 tbs Thyme

1 qt Heavy Cream Salt & pepper

Cut tomatoes and garlic in one half. Season with basil, oregano, salt, pepper, and thyme. Toss in olive oil. Pre-heat oven to 350 degrees, roast tomatoes, and garlic for 10-15 minutes. After roasting, place tomatoes and garlic in a large pot. Add cream, salt, and pepper. Simmer for 10-12 minutes. Blend together with hand blender or emulsifier. In a soup bowl, ladle tomato bisque into bowl. Garnish with parmesan and fresh parsley.

Cauliflower Bisque

2 Heads Cauliflower

4 Cups Vegetable Stock

2 tbsp Fresh Minced Garlic 1/2 White Onion

1 Cup Parmesan

2 tsp Lemon Zest

2 tsp Parsley & Thyme

2 Strips of Rendered Bacon Salt & pepper to taste

Pre-heat oven to 350 degrees. Cut cauliflower into smaller pieces on a sheet pan. Season cauliflower with salt and pepper. Place in oven for 12-15 minutes. In a large pot, render bacon until lightly brown. Add onions sauté both together. Add roasted cauliflower, lemon zest, parsley, thyme, and garlic to pot with onions and bacon. Pour vegetable stock into pot. Let simmer for 15-20 minutes then blend all together. Enjoy in a soup bowl garnished with a dollop of sour cream.

Mississippi Catfish Stew

1 of Cup onions

1 Cup of Celery

1 Cup of Carrots

1/4 Cup of Fresh Basil and Thyme 1 Can of Tomatoes

1 Cup of Water

1-2 9 to 12 oz. of Catfish

Cut catfish in small pieces. Sauté catfish in medium pan. Dice carrots, celery, and onions into one- inch cubes. Sauté for 2-4 minutes until cooked. Add crushed tomatoes, water, then season. Let simmer to 15-20 minutes. Finally add fish to pan. Simmer for 15-20 minutes. Add salt and pepper to taste. Serve in large soup bowl.

Back Home Vegetable Soup

15 oz Can of Tomato Sauce ½ Cup of Diced Tomatoes ½ Cup of Diced Carrots

1 Cup of Whole Corn

2 Cups of Cannellini Beans ½ Cup of Cut Okra

½ Cup of Red Bell Pepper 2 Cloves of Garlic

½ tsp of Red Pepper Flakes ½ Cup of Fresh Parsley

1 Cup of Cubed Potatoes

Dice carrots and bell peppers into ½ inch cuts, do the same for potatoes. Add both to sauté pan. Cook for 4-6 minutes until soft. Add can of tomato sauce and 3 cups water. Let simmer for 5-10 minutes. After letting simmer, continue to add the rest of the ingredients. Serve in large soup bowl.

ENTREES

Bourbon Peach Glaze Salmon

8 oz. Salmon

1/2 tsp. of Chipotle Powder

1 tsp. of Lemon Zest

1 tsp. of Rosemary

3/4 Cup of Honey

1 Fresh Sliced Peach

Pinch of Cayenne Pepper

2 Cups of Baby Spinach (sautéed) 1 Whole Shallot

Season salmon with salt, pepper, cayenne, and chipotle powder in a medium pan. Pour 1/2 tsp of olive oil warm on medium heat. Lay salmon face side down until golden brown. Flip fish after 3-4 minutes. Sear 3-4 minutes for a medium rare finish. Cut one whole peach into slices. Dice shallots. Add to small pan on medium heat with a one-inch stick of butter. Sauté until shallots and peaches are caramelized. Add honey and a 1/4 cup of water. Cook until sauce is thick. Wilt spinach over a low heat. Add salt and pepper to taste. On a round plate, place wilted spinach in the center. Place salmon on top. Pour sautéed peaches and sauce as a finish.

Bayou Catfish

4-7 9 oz. Catfish

1/2 Cup of Okra

1/2 Cup of Diced Green and Red Peppers 16-20 of Jumbo Shrimp

1/2 Cup of Chili Sauce

Dash of Hot Sauce

Salt & Pepper, Old Bay to Taste

1 tsp. Minced Garlic

Thoroughly dry catfish. Season with salt, pepper, and Old Bay. Preheat oven to 375 degrees. In a large pan, drizzle with olive oil on high heat. Bake fish for 10-12 mins. In a smaller pan, pour in sautéed shrimp. Add bell pepper. Cut okra and add chili sauce. Cook with 1/4 cup of water. Season with salt, pepper, old bay, a dash of hot sauce and minced garlic. Let cook for 5-10 minutes until shrimp are fully cooked and sauce is thick. Plate Catfish filets. Top with shrimp and chili sauce. Garnish with parsley.

Shrimp and Grits

16-20 Jumbo Shrimp

8 Slices of Bacon

4 tbsp. of nGarlic

4 Cups of Corn Grits

12 Cups of Chicken Stock 4 Dashes of Hot Sauce

6 tsp. of Lemon Juice

1 Cup of Heavy Cream

5 Cups of Cheddar Cheese Salt & Pepper to taste

1 tsp. of Cayenne Pepper

Preheat chicken stock and cream for 4-6 minutes until a rolling boil. Slowly stir in grits for 4-6 minutes until grits are fully cooked through. Add cheddar, salt, and pepper to grits. Continue to stir. Preheat pan to medium heat. Add 1/2 stick of butter, sauté shrimp, bacon, bell peppers and garlic together. Season with cayenne pepper, salt, and pepper to taste. Remove shrimp and bacon. Add 1/4 cup of stock to pan. Let sauce simmer until thick. In a large serving dish, pour in grits. Top with shrimp and bacon. Finish with sauce.

Mid- Delta Fried Quail

8 Whole Quails

4 Stocks of Leeks

4 Cans of Black Eye Peas 8 Slices of Cubed Bacon 2 Cups of Buttermilk

1 egg

4 Cups of flour

Clean and cut Quail in half. Season with salt, pepper, and cayenne pepper. In a container, pour in buttermilk and eggs. Whisk together. Add salt and pepper. In another container, add flour, season with salt and pepper. Dredge chicken in egg wash then coat with flour. Set pan to medium heat fry Quail for 8-10 minutes until golden brown. Cut leeks and bacon in one -inch slices then dump in a large pot. Add 1/4 stick of butter sauté leeks and bacon together until bacon is rendered. Continue to add black eye peas to pot. Gently stir ingredients together. On a large serving dish, place leeks, bacon, and black eye peas in the center. Place fried quails on top and garnish with parsley.

Rosedale Smothered Chicken

4 Pack Leg Quarters

6-8 Rooted Baby Carrots

1 Whole Jumbo Onion

6 Large Celery

2 Cups of Chicken Stock Salt & Pepper to Taste

4 tbsp of Minced Garlic Allspice Seasoning to taste 1/2 Cup of Flour

Wash leg quarters and lightly dry with towel. Season with all seasonings. In a large skillet, pour olive oil to coat the pan on a high heat. Pan sear leg quarters for 6-8 minutes, 4 minutes on both sides. Chop carrots, onions, and celery, add to skillet along with chicken. Bake for 10 -12 minutes in a 350-degree pre-heated oven. After 12 minutes remove chicken and vegetables. Add flour and 2 cups of chicken stock. Simmer until gravy is thick. Season with salt and pepper. On a large serving platter, place bed of vegetables in the center of plate. Top with chicken and finish with gravy.

DESSERTS

Strawberry Jam Cornbread

2 Boxes of Jiffy Mix

2 Eggs

2 Cups of milk

4 tbsp of butter (room temp) 2 Cups of fresh strawberries 2 tbsp of sugar

2 tbsp of strawberry jam

Cornbread Preparation: Set oven to 350 degrees, allow oven to preheat. In a cast iron skillet, add 2 tsp of butter, then use a tsp of the cornbread mix to sprinkle atop the butter in the middle of the skillet. Brown inside the oven for five minutes. (Will substitute oil in Jiffy cornbread recipe. This will add richness to the cornbread.)

Strawberry Jam Reduction: In a medium sized saucepan, melt three tbsps. of butter over medium heat. As bubbles appear, combine two cups of strawberries, two tbsp of sugar and two tbsp of strawberry jam. Allow to caramelize on low heat for four minutes. Let set for one minute.

Plating Your Southern Masterpiece: Remove cornbread from the oven, cut into even portions. Place a slice of cornbread on a plate. With a large spoon drizzle reduction over cornbread. Garnish with fresh strawberries and confectioner's sugar.

Flaky Biscuit Crust Peach Cobbler

2 Large Cans of Pillsbury Flaky Grands Biscuits 6 Pitted Beaches Split and Cut into 1/4's

1 Cup of Brown Sugar

1/2 Cup of White Sugar

2 tbsp of Butter

1 tsp of Cinnamon

Making the peach filling: In a medium pot, add butter on a low heat for two minutes. Add brown sugar, white sugar, and cinnamon. Add six pitted peaches, let simmer on a low heat for ten minutes.

With your first can of biscuits: Peel doughy biscuits in half. Place biscuit halves in a buttered casserole dish. Will serve as bottom crust.

Filling your cobbling: Pour peach filling over biscuit halves in dish about 3⁄4 full, allowing room for top crust. Place leftover biscuit halves over filling.

With your second can of biscuits: Peel biscuits in half. Fill gaps on the top layer with the rest of the halves.

Baking: Place cobbler in the oven. Cook at 365 degrees for 15-20 minutes. **Serving:** Cut into squares and garnish with brown and white sugar.

Banana Foster Banana and Southern Comfort Pudding

1 1⁄2 tbsps. of butter
6 Bananas (thinly chopped)
1⁄2 Cup of Brown Sugar
2 Shots of Southern Comfort
2 Cups of Whipped Cream
1 Cup of Blackburn's Molasses (any pure sugar cane will work)
2 Packets of Instant Banana Pudding Mix

Sautee the bananas in melted butter, add molasses. Add whiskey along with two chopped bananas. Bring to a bubble. Allow to simmer on low for ten minutes.

Let cool. Add to banana pudding mx. Add whip cream and four chopped bananas. Follow directions on pudding box.

Line the bottom of a glass dish with vanilla cookies. Layer pudding atop layer of cookies, filling dish halfway. Add another layer of cookies. Add another layer of pudding. Top with whipped cream.

Flash Fiction

UMBRELLAS UNDER GAZEBOS

There are two kinds of women in this world. Women who pray and women who judge. The woman who prays has seen enough, while the woman who judges has seen nothing. The woman who prays has God's favor, while the woman who judges presumes herself as God. The woman who judges looks at the woman who prays and thinks she should wear longer skirts, while it is she who tends to entertain another woman's husband. The woman who prays is not afraid to admit her wrongs. The one who judges thinks that praying is the bowing of her head when the preacher says so. She is at the church doors as soon as they open, scouring the congregation looking for the next praying woman to pick apart.

The praying woman is humble, she even smiles and hugs the judging woman when church is done. The judging woman hugs back but it is as disingenuous as Lucifer when he roamed the Kingdom of Heaven. The praying woman knows that God forgives even the most execrable mistakes, but a judging woman solemnly believes in hell. A judging woman is superior to "worldly" endeavors. The praying woman, though she is not perfect, has the fortitude to forgive a judging woman.

Somewhere in the Delta, deep down in the southern south, there is a judging woman billowing a Baptist church with her self-righteous bitterness. On the other hand, is a righteous woman proudly walking in her purpose. Just after the rain, you can find a judging woman standing under a gazebo with an umbrella over her head in the dead middle of the sun looking, watching, waiting for the next praying woman to pass her by.

THE HALLWAY

1979, in a hallway that seemed to never end, the carpet damp from a leaking roof and the erosion of time, sat a woman, a black woman peeling paint from the wall with her fingernails. With nowhere to go and no place to be, she faced the wall, holding the bottom of her womb, glancing away to a portrait on the wall for as long as time would allow. The portrait was of a man, a black man, who sat on a shot-gun house porch holding a rifle between his legs, his left hand on his knee. He had a slight smile as he stared back at the woman in the hallway for hours, never looking away. She grew tired, sitting Indian style on the carpet, disregarding the blood and lead under her nails.

She had thick lips that was the foundation of a pronounced cupid's bow, a broad nose and an afro crowning her head that hadn't been tended to in a month's time. The woman wore a necklace made of wood and an army broach that was a representation of America. Her checkered blue and white dress fell below her knees whether if she was standing or sitting. Blood from her fingernails had turned the bottom of her dress a new color. Next to her was a pack of cigarettes and a box of matches that was also tinged of blood. She sat there holding the bottom of her womb, rocking back and forth, staring at the portrait of the man holding the shotgun who wore a slight smile. He never took his eyes away from the strange woman in the long hallway who sat scraping the white of off the wall, painting it red.

THE WIDOWER

The latchkey kids would watch Mr. Sam Ellis walk down the sidewalk on his cane every afternoon around the same time. Instead of the children referring to him as Mr. Ellis, they would shout, "Sad Mane Sam!" It was a fact. Mr. Ellis was a sad, old man. See, fact is he didn't have a wife to grow old and die with. They all died early!

When Mr. Ellis was young, he had 3 lovely wives! They all died, although he didn't kill them, well on purpose.

Say he was rough! A womanizing, tall dark piece of handsome with white piano keys for teeth; Sam's daddy was a mixed man. White and Negro. Sam came out black as I don't know what, but that hair was fine as cat hair. Sam had women here, had women there, women everywhere!

But Sam got tired of leaping from one woman to another, so he went out to find him a woman to marry.

Miss Julie Anne Segar was Sam's first wife. Say she was high yellow with straight like hair! She had a pointed little nose like a white woman from down there in Louisiana. They say she had Portuguese running all up and through her blood. Come from a good family too! A decent well put together woman. She never had kids, but she was a real pretty schoolteacher where she considered her students her own. She loved kids. She was begging Mr. Ellis to give her a baby. He was trying! Lord knows he was! She just couldn't seem to get pregnant for him. Come to find out Mr. Ellis had given Miss Julie Anne a bad venereal disease that scarred her womanhood. She could never have kids. They say Mr. Ellis gave a real chocolate woman a baby, though.

The baby looked like Sam spit her out himself! Guess Miss Julie Anne couldn't take it. They say she got so depressed she walked in the river! When they found her pretty body, she was blue almost. Now Sam knows he knew better.

Sam cried about two days. Before Miss Julie was even in the ground good, he was moved in with that chocolate woman that had the baby his former wife couldn't. Now he made this new woman his wife! Her name was Miss Henrietta Jeanette Downs, and she was one hell of a woman. He took the ring from Miss Julie's finger and put it on Henrietta's! See Miss Henrietta was a strong black woman and that's what Mr. Sam loved so much about her. She was tall and had mocha skin with not a blemish in sight! She was thin but curvy. A sight for sore eyes whenever she wore a form fitting dress! All the brothers wanted to give her babies, but she only let Sam Ellis do it. Such a beautiful woman! But one thing Miss Henrietta ain't know was that Sam started gambling bad after Miss Julie died. He had even started gambling bill money! One day the lights got turned off! Sam was gone all times of night in the alley over at Juke Saw's joint shooting dice, arguing with uptown brothers. So, one night Miss Henrietta was so fed up that she went storming down there to the joint, mad as a white man cut off by a black man in traffic. But little did she know Mr. Sam had been cheating some northern boys out of some money and they weren't too happy about it. Miss Henrietta walked right in the crossfire! Shot and killed right there in that very alley way.

Now we all know Sam don't waste no time. He was moved in with that fast gal that work over in the bar at Juke Saw's Joint, him, and his baby! She was dumb enough to let him, too! Poor Chile ain't have no common sense and no mama to teach her none either! Her name was Miss Louise Johnson, say she kin to the blues player, Robert Johnson. She was younger than his two widows. She was pretty but ain't have much breast or hips. She had real long hair, though, and a smile that would knock you back out of the door. She was brown and short to the ground. He ain't marry her though. He just made her raise his baby until that child was half grown! That baby was calling Miss Louise, Mama! She even stayed with Miss Louise when Sam Ellis met Miss Rita Jenkins. Miss Jenkins was a mature woman! She was an albino woman from up there in Chicago! Well educated woman! She practiced law and made good money too!

See, Sam was a carpenter, but he was getting older, and his knees was starting to hurt. He smooth talked Miss Jenkins with all that southern audacity, right on up in her two - story home. He still had the ring from his first and second marriage and damn it, it was going to be his third wife's ring too. But now, while Miss Jenkins would work, Mr. Ellis had Miss Louise all in her house! The daughter too! One day Miss Jenkins came home early and found Sam and Miss Louise getting down in her bed! See, Miss Jenkins couldn't handle too much excitement. She had a heart condition that caused her to have a heart attack as soon as she realized what she was seeing! Miss Jenkins fell dead right there in her master bedroom. Miss Louise left running and ain't never look back. Say she took off to California and became a hippie! Sam was left right in the Delta with a 14-year-old daughter who was fast as hell! Child got pregnant when she was 15 and had another when she was 17!

Sam was too old by now to find another wife, so he just tended to his grandbabies in Miss Jenkins house! The courts gave it to him since she never had kids and was naive enough to add his name to the deed after they said, 'I do".

All the older single women around town knew all about Sam Ellis and his tricks. Nobody gave him time no more! His daughter got a degree and took her kids to Memphis! She said she wasn't about to be looking behind no old man, no way in hell! Sam had a stroke not too long after his daughter left him. He had to live in a nursing home for a while until his long-lost sister agreed to take care of him, but only for financial benefits, though.

He could walk! But his mouth was twisted, and you could barely understand what he was saying! His sister slapped him when she couldn't understand him and made him sit on the porch when she had company.

So, he walked on his cane everyday down Avenue G, past the latchkey kids.

They laughed and pointed, "Look at old sad mane Sam! Slobbing from the mouth!"

THE WOMEN

The Southern women of The Delta wore oversized floppy hats and their dresses hung past the knee. Grand beings of wisdom and great gesture, talking with their hands in ways only one from the Delta would understand. Those who loved God were closest to heaven, they all esteemed. They were grounded like the cotton that sprouted up from the alluvial Mississippi Delta soil. They met after church on Sunday for apple dumplings and sweet- as-you-could-take-it iced tea. There were white women. There were fair skinned women as well as cocoa-colored ones. They were all beautiful, individually. Yet, when they gathered and became one, they were strikingly the most gorgeous sight under God's pillowed skies and its silver lining. Each had a specific talent. Some could cook. Some could draw. A few could write poems, and a few were best at gossip. But on Sunday, when they all gathered in a barren field under the sunshine in the Delta, there was love. There was unity. Did not matter the color of skin.

DELTA NIGHT

Miss Ida Fae, standin' there in the kitchen combin' naps out from her head—hair so thick one of the teeth from the comb flew up to Neptune. But oh, Miss Ida Fae was pretty. Don't know where she gets that pretty from. Maybe she go way back. 'Cuz her mama, Sue, wasn't no good-lookin' woman. Miss Ida Fae's daddy was an ole ugly mane, but they had beautiful souls, guess that's all that matters. They call him Mr. Alley. Look like a mule hauling in from the fields 'round six every night— Just wo' down. But Miss Ida Fae be real pretty with a head full of nappy, thick hair.

Miss Ida Fae had them skinny black legs with a real slim behind. Her bust spilled over the two bras she owned, but maybe they was just too little. She ain't have not one bit of stomach! Flat down to the bone! Flat like that Delta land she was livin' on. And boy, them cheekbones was high up to heaven! She was real, real black like the Delta night— pretty and as chocolate as she could be. So pretty that all the white boys would be standin' and spittin' and watching Miss Ida Fae 'til she outta sight. She loved it too. You know, now to think 'bout it, I ain't never seen Miss Ida Fae lookin' at no black boy, let alone talkin' to one! Miss Ida Fae act like she a virgin! But she ain't look it! Not the way them bust grew in the past year! Two big melons on that tiny chest of hers! But guess that don't mean nothin'. Mrs. Sue, Ida Fae's mama, bust just like that too. Maybe why that's why Mr. Alley been in love so many years. He just as happy and content as he could be.

Now Miss Ida Fae loved her some church on Sunday. Just like a Delta woman. She used to be so excited to go to church to praise the Lord with all the other young women at Living Grove Pentecostal Church on the side of a dirt road in Drew, Mississippi. Yep, Miss Ida Fae right outta Drew, born and raised. She was raised up in that church too. All them handsome Black boys after Miss Ida Fae at church. Even the Preacher's boy—crazy 'bout Miss Ida Fae. But she always acted like she had to go home. Knowin' damn well she ain't have to go nowhere! She grown! One time the preacher boy followed her home, and she took off to runnin' like somebody was gone take her! It was the middle of the 60s, so Miss Ida Fae combed and combed that nappy hair of hers until was a big afro sitting on top her head. Looked like a wig!

Now Miss Ida Fae was nineteen goin' on 20 with no Mr. and no babies. Think she liked that too. Miss Ida Fae liked her freedom. Miss Ida Fae was a hard worker, now. She was workin' over at the hospital in Cleveland as an aid wiping behinds for a livin'. She said she was gone go to Delta State for nursin', but what negro you know went to nursin' school at a white college in Mississippi? Maybe some, but they weren't letting negroes get too far in the Delta back then.

Ida Fae said she gone be a nurse, so guess she was close to it workin' that job.

Don't think all white folks was bad in the Delta, now. Ida Fae was smart and pretty with a lot goin' for herself. This white lady, one of her patients took to Miss Ida Fae. She told Miss Ida Fae that she had a nephew over in Arkansas that loved negro women. Say he a good man with a little money put away. When white folks say little, we know they mean a lot! Say he was gone sell the small piece of land he had if he could find him a black woman to move off up north with. But he just ain't want any negro woman. Say he want a real black one. One black as the Delta night. Say he ain't want no high yella black woman! He said it ain't make no sense! He may as well be with a white woman! So, the old white lady had the audacity to tell Miss Ida Fae that she was black like the Delta night, and she would be perfect for him. She said she wouldn't have to even bit mo' work no mo'! Guess what? Miss Ida Fae had the audacity to say she wanted to meet him! Ain't never give no colored boy the time of day! Guess you can't blame her. All a colored boy wanted a woman for is cookin' and cleanin' and layin on her back—he didn't care how a woman feel. Guess this here white man was gone take good care of Miss Ida Fae, according to what her patient said. And you know what? He sho' did. Ida Fae call herself gettin' fancy one weekend summer evening in the Delta. That hair was sitting like a big fro wig on that pretty head of hers. She had on a white dress with them long black legs showin' off—glistenin' in that Delta sun. That white showed up good on her skin too—made the dress jump out at ya. She did a good job pickin' that one. And she did a good job pickin' her man 'cuz he sho' was a fine one. He was a tall handsome white mane. He had that blonde hair and sky blue eyes. He was sweet as lemon meringue pie on a sunny Sunday.

First time he visited Miss Ida Fae, Mrs. Sue and Mr. Alley was scared as a fool thinkin' he came for some trouble. Instead, he brought Mrs. Sue some yellow flowers and some chocolate, and Ida Fae too. He fell in love with Miss Ida Fae time he laid them blue eyes on her. Miss Ida Fae was a little shy but that white man made her light up. Reckon Mrs. Sue and Mr. Alley ain't mind they daughter coatin' no white boy 'cuz he was down there every Sunday evening to see Miss Ida Fae. Livin' in the Delta, couldn't no white man and no black woman be in peace in public. Somebody was gone get shot and hung! So, Mr. Pete Bill Outlaw came to see Miss Ida Fae in her mama and daddy's shed 'hind they small house until he asked her to be his wife. She said yes.

"Baby I'm gone sell my land and we can elope in Nevada, then we go raise some babies up north. What you think, my beautiful?"

Mr. Pete Bill loved him some Ida Fae. Miss Ida Fae loved her some Pete Bill, but she loved Mrs. Sue and Mr. Alley too. She said she was gone marry him, but she said she had to pray on leavin'. Mr. Pete Bill Outlaw loved Miss Ida Fae so much that he understood, and he gave her some time. For three weeks Miss Ida Fae was fastin' and prayin' up a storm. A real storm came to water Mr. Alley few crops they had, and things had started growin'. Miss Ida Fae say that was her sign from God. She knew God was gone take care of Mrs. Sue and Mr. Alley. She could go on and be a good man's wife! She could go on and be a good wife!

Mr. Pete musta been readin' Miss Ida Fae's mind 'cuz here he come kickin' up Delta dust down the road.

"I couldn't take it no more, baby. I had to see your pretty face." He gave Ida Fae a hug ain't nobody ever gave her.

Miss Ida Fae said yes again, and she packed her one bag she had that her cousin from Illinois left. It was blue and big with hardly nothin' in it, but that's okay. Mr. Pete Bill loved Miss Ida Fae anyhow.

Miss Ida Fae kissed Mrs. Sue and Mr. Alley goodbye. She said goodbye to the Delta night too 'cuz they drove straight on to Vegas.

"Baby, you gonna love all the lights. I can't wait to see you light up. You gonna be my Mrs. Outlaw."

They drove and drove and drove. Seemed like the road never ended. There was no end to the sun. Guess both loved them some Delta night 'cuz neither was restin' easy in the hotel in New Mexico. But Miss Ida Fae sho' ate good.

She liked the food there but she missed the Delta catfish Mr. Alley caught in those Delta ponds.

So, they finally got to Vegas, and she heard the music all loud and people playin' rock and roll. She liked the music, but she missed the Delta blues playing in the Delta joint. Mr. Pete Bill loved him some Ida Fae. He'd do anything for that black Queen. So, Miss Ida Fae said, *"Bill, baby. I love you. But I love the Delta, too. We just gone* have to put the bitter with the sweet and buy some land there and I be yo wife on it." Mr. Pete, like the angel he was, just smiled.

So, Miss Ida Fae became Mrs. Ida Fae Outlaw right there in Las Vegas, Nevada. She was now a white man's wife.

Mr. Outlaw had money so it ain't matter where they lived. But Mrs. Ida Fae ain't like no big city so she begged and begged to go back to The Delta.

Mr. Outlaw took her. She watched the clouds in the big sky while Mr. Pete was drivin' cross America for his new bride. The clouds were like cotton in a Delta field way up in the great above.

He bought some land back behind where Mrs. Sue and Mr. Alley lived, just in case she needed somewhere to hide. You should have seen it, Mrs. Ida Fae Outlaw's nightgown dragging in the night between the alley way to Mr. Outlaw house. She carried a lantern and boy could she walk fast. Fastest walkin' black woman ever seen.

She'd go make love to Mr. Outlaw in the night real, real good like she done it before. She was a virgin 'til she married Mr. Pete Bill—that dark skin up 'gainst that milky white skin. Mrs. Ida was knocked up now. Gone be white lookin' like his pappy with some kinky hair! But bet he beautiful like them both.

Just sho' he was. Big ol fat baby boy. They named him Oliver.

Mrs. Ida Fae fannin' that round baby up there on Mrs. Sue and Mr. Alley's porch. Jumpin' that baby up and down on them narrow hips, Mrs. Ida Fae Outlaw—cheekbones high to the sky. Face so pretty with a head full of nappy ass hair. The baby's head of hair wasn't as kinky, but he was gone need a pressin' soon. Blonde and kinky like, but the nice kinky. Mr. Alley planted some greens and cabbage and he tended to 'em the whole season. Pete Bill love Mr. Alley, so he brought him a cold glass of water from time to time. But one time the wrong person saw Mr. Pete Bill bein' nice to Mr. Alley. A young white boy drivin' down the dirt road lookin' and bein' nosey. Ida Fae standin' in a distance bouncin' that baby of Pete Bill's on her narrow hips. That white boy saw that too! *"Pete Bill! Thank he gone go tellin' somebody? Thank he know this here baby is yours?"*, said Mr. Alley.

Pete Bill looked over at Mrs. Ida Fae Outlaw and smiled. He kneeled and took the empty glass from Mr. Alley and he asked him what he was makin' for dinner 'cause Oliver was cuttin' some teeth and he could gum down on some cabbage greens. You could see the tears shootin' down Mrs. Ida Fae's eyes. See Mr. Pete Bill was quiet with his feelings. He never let a soul know how he really felt!

That night, Mrs. Ida Fae was makin' love to Mr. Pete Bill like she never did before! He made love back just the same. Gettin' lost in that Delta night made them months fly by! Whew! Oliver already walkin' and Mrs. Ida Fae belly stuck out with another one! Mrs.Ida Fae—little ol bitty thang but stomach stuck out far as the west! She had a beautiful, fat gal this time and she had that good hair like Pete Bill! Prettiest baby anyone ever seen. She named her Sue Lilly.

One day Mr. Pete Bill rode over to Isola to pick up some fertilizer from a farmer he met in Indianola. Mr. Pete Bill turned the rest of that land into some crops 'cause that's the only way you could survive in the Delta, off the land back then. That farmer's son was the same boy drivin' through Drew lookin' and bein nosey! Small world! Even smaller Delta. Pete Bill ain't know for sure but he had a hunch. He knew somethin' wasn't right! That young boy stared at Mr. Pete Bill like he lost somethin' off his face! But like I said, Mr. Pete Bill real quiet. You never know what was on his mind! He smiled and gave the farmer his money and he loaded his truck up and went home.

"Daddy! He lives over in Drew and I could've sworn I saw him bein' way too nice to some negroes. Then there was a negro woman standin' there holdin' a baby that looked half white! Reckon it's his baby? You gonna have to come see for yourself, daddy!" The farmer frowned. The boy must've been evil, or somethin' cause was real happy 'bout doin' something "bout it". Mr. Pete Bill was far from stupid! He used to be an army man, so he knew when something wasn't right! He drove down that dusty Delta road all the way to Drew thinkin'. He got home and he walked right up to Mrs. Sue and Mr. Alley small shack house, and he said real real calm, *"Mrs. Ida, my wife, we got to go and we got to go now."* Miss Ida Fae ain't waste no time packin' up their things and getting the babies together. *"Mr. Alley, I'm gone leave you three hundred dollars and some fertilizer for them crops out there. You hire you a hand if you can't keep it up alone. I'm gone take your daughter up North. She will be safer with me, and the babies will be safer. Come on, Ida Fae."*

See, Mr. Pete Bill was a real smart man. He used his instinct! He put Mrs. Ida

Fae in that truck of his and he put them babies in right behind her. By that time, it was getting to be dark. They took off in the Delta night—

the same road them boys was comin' to take Pete Bill away from Mrs. Ida Fae.

They had sheets on, and they were burning torches, ridin' horses, and made Mrs. Sue and Mr. Alley get up out they bed! They looked high and low for Mr. Pete Bill but he was long gone in The Delta night. They set a tree on fire and left.

Some help from down the road ran down to help Mr. Alley put the fire out. Mr. Alley was just thankin' God 'cause he knew if Mr. Pete Bill ain't come home and take his daughter, them Klansman was gone do somethin' real serious. He was thankin' God! Mr. Pete Bill drove until it wasn't night or Delta no more. They ended up in Cincinnati, Ohio, and that's where they stayed— a small country town where hardly, anybody lived. Mrs. Ida Fae drew pictures of Sue Lilly and Oliver and sent them down to Mrs. Sue and Mr. Alley. She took pictures and sent them too!

Mr. Alley died some years later. Not too soon after, Mrs. Sue passed away too. They say she missed her little old husband so much. Guess it's true that someone can die from a broken heart.

Mr. Pete Bill loved Mrs. Ida Fae for the rest of his life. He put her through nursing school, and she became a real nurse! Sue Lilly and Oliver grew up and married off. Oliver married a red headed black woman! She yellow as the sun! Pale and pretty— freckles scattered over her face like fire ants. Sue Lilly married a real dark chocolate black mane that was mean as a snake, but she loved him.

Mr. Pete Bill developed cancer and died. Wasn't even 50 yet. Mrs. Ida Fae was strong, but she couldn't handle being alone and away from the Delta soil. She moved back down to Mississippi and was nursing in the Delta! She was a great nurse too. She wasn't wipin' behinds no more! She was takin' blood and talkin' to the doctors! She was savin' lives. She moved back on the land she grew up on. She bought a horse too since it was too much land not to. Sue Lilly divorced that mean mane of hers, so she and her brown babies made their way back to The Delta too, livin' with Mrs. Ida Fae. Mrs. Ida grew old watchin' her grandbabies grow up like she did her two babies. As time went on, Sue Lilly's babies was having babies. Sue Lilly remarried and was happier than a bunny on an Easter Sunday. Mrs. Ida Fae could still smell Pete Bill's scent and the way his narrow nose brushed against her voluptuous lips. She thought of him every day, every day up until she died on her land in the middle of a Delta Night.

B IS FOR BALTIMORE

B is the most honest letter in the alphabet. B for Black, a euphemism for the word beautiful, just like Baltimore.

Town folk always pestered her about her name, asking why her mother named her Baltimore, when she was born and raised in Panther Burn, Mississippi—down Highway 61. The highway boasted The Mississippi Delta land and if you wanted to see the most beautiful thing in the world, just keep driving. Everything was yellow like the sun that shine down on it, the corn mazes that you dare not get lost in, and the bountiful sunflower beds full of wild bees. Men working on the side of the road, wiping sweat from their dark foreheads, stopping to watch the cars fly by. B was for Baltimore but some of the unlucky fellas thought it was for Bitch when they tried to get after Miss Baltimore. *My mama named me Baltimore cause that's where she said the man she got me by from. Now get the hell on.* Snappy woman, she was, typical Delta woman with a little meat on her bones. Some say she big-boned but her mee-maw say she borderline obese, just like her whole family—but she was a fine sister with those bodacious hips. Baltimore was raised on good cooking and soul food her whole life, so it was a shame to the old folks that she made 32 with all those childbearing hips and ain't had not one baby. Old folks say something was wrong with her, but Baltimore wasn't no baby making factory. She was an educated woman who taught school part time at a community college in Leflore County, even though she talked like she was raised on a plantation when she was at home. She was one of the first colored women to teach on a college level in the Delta, but it was all 'cause she was high yellow. She couldn't pass for white though. Her nose was round and pronounced and she owned a set of huge breast, with that Aunt Jemima shape of hers. Everybody used to wonder why Miss Baltimore wasn't married. Plenty men loved Baltimore—negroes falling at her feet. Don't get it twisted! She used to be turning them men down fast as they would come knocking at her door. Soon as they knock, she opened it and slammed it right back! Baltimore was a bold woman. She knew what she wanted. She knew she ain't want no man who was after any pretty woman he come by. One brother got mad and started a rumor at the barber shop on the edge of town. *"Say she likin' on gals and don't want nothing to do with no brothers one bit!"* One of the older men in a jazzy blue hat and green checkered overalls, smoking a cigar in the corner blurted out, *"You just mad cause none of you negros ain't good enough."*

A FIELD OF SUNFLOWERS

I once grew a field of sunflowers, for two reasons, for the beauty and for the doves. I planted my seeds by the end of March. I stood over them and watered them every day. By fall, the plants had begun to water me.

The Delta sun hung from the sky, real low to the flat land. I had never seen land flat as the land in the Mississippi Delta.

Fall

I bought a rusty 'ol shotgun from an old man who had shot many a'dove in his day. He said it had the luck of the dove on it.

Maybe I was special, I guess. He sold it to me for thirty dollars and a bag of pennies I had been collecting since I was nine.

Sunflower Co. 6:29A.M

I could see doves fly down, diving headfirst for a sunflower to be among.

I cocked back my pistol over my petite shoulder, and I aimed it at one sitting perfectly on a stem. Finger on the trigger, eye on the prize, and then I just couldn't.

I once had a cousin—, same name as mine, same birthday too. She was the kind of bold soul who hid behind who she wanted to be. She lived vicariously through anyone brave or beautiful. I can remember her smile. It too, was like the sun hanging in the Delta sky. My great- grandfather and her great- grandfather had been brothers living in Money,

Mississippi, decades before we were born. She was 10 years my elder, but she felt to be more of a sister than a cousin. We had been close, closer than we ever were in previous years. She was recovering from an exhausting marriage with four small children to show for it.

Everything about her was majestic, I must say. No matter what she was facing, she always wore a smile accompanied by a sweet spirit. A legion was attached to our family, constant spirals of depression. We all knew this and some of suffered more than others. Unfortunately, she would succumb.

It was a new week; a telephone call would come—it was news of my dearest cousin. She had been found not breathing. She had died of an overdose. I couldn't cry or feel the emotions I needed to because I had begun to take antidepressants. The Legion had begun to get the best of me, I refused to allow myself to lose.

I fought back. I faced it, and then I came out of darkness, for a short time at least.

I had always had dreams of growing my own sunflower field. So, I did just that, for two reasons. One reason was for the beauty, and one was for the doves.

I just drug my shotgun out there in case some hunter was standing over in the woods hunting for my precious doves.

Maybe I was the only one in The Delta who didn't hunt the doves in my own field. I never ever allowed other hunters to hunt them there either. I had experienced enough death to be causing it myself. The doves reminded me of my cousin, pure as the color white and meek as baby Jesus in his manger.

$5,000 fine and warm a bullet for those caught hunting doves in my sunflower field. The doves kept the Legion away.

ANGELS IN MISSISSIPPI

Chewing on straw, a chunky gut fellow sipping from an ol' Coca Cola glass bottle— You know? The kind made in the 50's.

He asked me questions like, "Where you from, gal?"

I said, "another time." And indeed, I was. While they were standing there, they stood in silence like they were candidly waiting for time to lapse. I had gotten lost in the country on my way home.

The kind of lost where the only thing in sight was an old broken-down gas station and trees for miles. That's where I found them, "Jim's."

The paint on the building wasn't white anymore, it was chipped away, decade by decade. No gas for me, not like I needed any anyways, if I did need it, the pumps were rusted over. Dirty overalls, dirty boots, and such. *"Y'all mind if I take a picture?"*, I asked.

Their eyes answered me, no words spoken.

I took a picture with an instant polaroid camera, but there was nothing there but that old broken-down gas station once it developed.

That was the day that I met some Mississippi Angels.

BELLE OF THE BLUES BALL

Ain't no blues better than the blues in the Delta, Belle of the blues ball — she was.

All the brothers, all the men, all the boys watchin' this luscious Black woman be black and proud. Twirling hips and moving her lips to the words.

The sadness, the joy, the blues.

Young boys slidin' under tables just to look at those clean white cotton underwear under her short A-line dress.

She would say, *"They ain't have no business in here anyways."*

"You from by the countryside ain't, you gal?" A brave man asked. She'd reply, *"Yes! And what of it?"* *"What side of country you from, gal?"* She'd reply, *"The side of let me be in peace, now scat cat!"*

The man said, *"I like pretty country bitches with quick mouths."*

She said, *"Don't know who you callin' a bitch, but a bitch sholl ain't what I be!* So, she kept dancing, dancing all night. Dancing until her feet hurt, dancing until she got it right. Nothing them brothers could do! But watch and pray.

Just praying that one day she wouldn't be so hard on a mane! *"The blues make ya sad!"*, one mane hollered! Miss Belle will too.

MICKET'S LOUNGE

The Mississippi Delta was the third stone from the sun and the fire had created the blues. The blues reminded me of my uncle. His sadness and how he and the Blues had soul ties. Even the trees could feel the sorrow of the Blues, there in the Delta. The Delta was the soul and the blues was the body it lived in.

Mitcket's Lounge sat on the corner of Scott Street and Carrollton Avenue. I remember how my aunt looked in the photo that night at Mitcket's Lounge. Rouge lips, rouge cheeks, smoked out eyes and a fully blossomed head of hair. It was her Mississippi Delta, as beautiful as she was. She wore a black floral spaghetti strapped dress with pink and yellow wildflowers that bore her cinnamon brown shoulders.

I imagined the air in Mitcket's Lounge. The taste of smoke and how it danced in the air— blue hues illuminated smoke shadows juxtaposed outward towards the sky, confined by a tin ceiling.

Women centered the dance floor. They bruised the atmosphere with hips swaying dangerously back and forth, from the ferocious spell from the blues. Fuchsia lips glossing under strobe lights. I wondered if my aunt loved the blues as much as my uncle, because I know she never got up to dance, she wasn't the kind of woman to dance. My uncle was the man behind a booth with big headphones taking requests from the people of Micket's Lounge. Stormy Mondays with Albert King, Delta folks spent at Micket's Lounge. "Love That Burns" by Fleetwood Mac played as my uncle watched my aunt as she sat bashfully in a distant corner, I imagine. She wouldn't entertain other men, not because she was stuck up, but because she was afraid of how hungry they looked when she would notice them gazing. But I imagine my uncle made her feel a certain kind of safe where she wasn't frightened by his stares.

My aunt, the most beautiful, smiling and blushing at camera flash. My aunt was electric back then in the 80s, electric as a thunderstorm strike. I see why he fell for the most beautiful woman in Micket's Lounge when he knew better, because he loved the blues. He knew that the men who sang the blues wept about women like my aunt, who were beautiful and mysterious, enough to make a man afraid to love.

PHILOPHOBIA

I never had a brother, and I never really had a grandfather.
All I had was a coal-colored man who I kept at the back of
my mind. I didn't need a man all in my bed breathing over
me, trying to own me—nobody owned me but God. I kept
this in mind, because me? I liked to learn from other folk's
mistakes. My mother's voice echoed over the phone; she
told me her stepfather had passed. I never met him; he lived
in Chicago. I had heard of him all while I was growing up.
I remember my grandmother saying that back in the '70s,
he would sit at the foot of the bed, rolling a joint and would
smoke every morning until his nose ran. She also told me
about the many times she would have to see the doctor to
be cured from venereal diseases he'd given her. Looking
at old photos, he was a rather handsome man. Slim, tall
and had a healthy afro, two shades lighter than brown. I
remember my mother telling me that once that her father
had disappeared and this one did too after so long. So as
for me, I didn't want a man all in my bed, breathing over me
trying to own me—nobody owned me but God.

MISSISSIPPI IS GOD'S COUNTRY

Signs painted and pointed to fresh grown blueberries— the Delta sun looking down over God's country—The Mississippi Delta. You must get through the mazes to get to Vicksburg by route from Greenwood—fresh blueberry fields along the way. Hair sticking to the sides of my face melting in the smothering Delta heat. There was no space between the sky, sun, and the pavement— black pavement that looked like black water leading to nowhere. The Delta, was God's country, made special in its own way. You know how the believers, believe? Make your pain your purpose! So, God gave The Mississippi Delta some pain. The black folks, some white folks too, took their fingers and soul and made some tunes then called it "The Blues". Grandmothers took their fingers and mashed together greens and cornbread then called it soul food. A place that should be called God's Country, but somehow, someone, made it The Mississippi Delta.

The End

www.ingramcontent.com/pod-product-compliance
Lightning Source LLC
Chambersburg PA
CBHW051728050726
47598CB00003B/1091